CCSS Genre **Expository Text**

Essential Question
How are living things adapted to their environment?

CAVE CREATURES

by Jocelyn Cranefield

INTRODUCTION

Caves are found in every part of the world. These natural openings in the ground may extend far beyond their entrance and go deep beneath Earth's surface. At first sight, a cave might seem to be only a dark and empty space, and if you shine your flashlight around inside the cave, you'll probably just see emptiness. However, it's likely that if you go inside the cave, you won't be alone.

Scientists who study the **organisms** in caves— biospeleologists—know these places are teeming with life.

Caves can be located on the coast, within a forest, or even beneath a desert. Some are made out of limestone, while others have been formed from marble or lava. Some caves are full of exquisite stone formations, and others are full of smelly, poisonous gases. However, the world's caves all have one thing in common— they're a **haven** for many different animals.

Lechuguilla Cave in New Mexico is famous for its beautiful mineral formations.

Michael Nichols/National Geographic Stock

Some of these animals are only visitors to the cave, while others are permanent residents. These creatures come in some very surprising forms. Many of them have distinctive adaptations to help them survive in the challenging environment of a cave. Adaptations are the special characteristics that enable a living thing to survive in certain conditions.

CAVES OF ALL SIZES

Explorers have identified more than 50,000 natural caves in the world. Some of these caves are single tunnels or caverns, but others are massive systems of interconnected underground spaces. The deepest known cave is the Krubera Cave, near the Black Sea, which is at least 7,188 feet deep. Compare its depth with the heights of some tall buildings, below. The world's longest cave is the Mammoth Cave system in Kentucky. It is a limestone **labyrinth** that extends for more than 350 miles underground.

The Krubera Cave

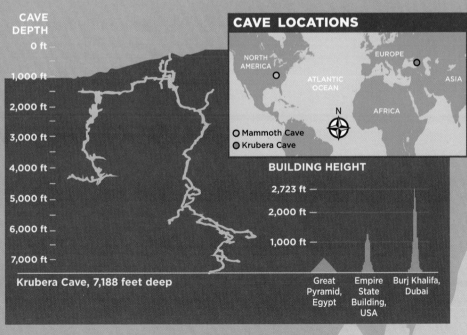

CAVE DEPTH

0 ft —

1,000 ft —

2,000 ft —

3,000 ft —

4,000 ft —

5,000 ft —

6,000 ft —

7,000 ft —

Krubera Cave, 7,188 feet deep

CAVE LOCATIONS

NORTH AMERICA

EUROPE

ATLANTIC OCEAN

ASIA

AFRICA

N

O Mammoth Cave
O Krubera Cave

BUILDING HEIGHT

2,723 ft —

2,000 ft —

1,000 ft —

Great Pyramid, Egypt

Empire State Building, USA

Burj Khalifa, Dubai

CHAPTER ONE

FROM THE ENTRANCE TO THE TWILIGHT ZONE

As the sun sets, these bats emerge from their cave to hunt.

Some animals, such as bats, skunks, raccoons, and snakes, visit caves only for shelter or to sleep. They stay near the cave entrance, where temperatures may be warmer in winter and cooler in summer than the outside environment. These animals are called trogloxenes, or cave visitors. Trogloxenes spend just a part of their lives in caves. They can't survive without returning to the outside world to get food.

At certain times, caves may be densely populated by these creatures. On summer nights, up to 20 million Mexican free-tailed bats fly out of the Bracken Cave in Texas. They make a swarm so dense that it shows up on a nearby airport's radar!

The Mexican free-tailed bat is a trogloxene. It is **nocturnal** and spends the day roosting in **colonies** that hang from cave roofs. At dusk it flies out of the cave to catch and eat insects.

4

Fred Bruemmer/Photolibrary/Getty Images

Like most other bats, the Mexican free-tailed bat has a special adaptation called echolocation. This adaptation helps it navigate in the dark cave. The bat emits high-pitched squeaking sounds and then listens for an echo with its massive ears. It uses the echo to find out the locations of things around it.

In some places, bats hibernate in caves during the winter months. If disturbed, a hibernating bat may not live through the winter because its stored energy gets used up all at once. However, bats don't spend the entire winter asleep. They usually wake up from their dormant state for short periods about every 15 to 30 days. The place where a bat hibernates is called a hibernaculum.

In really cold climates, bears sometimes spend the winter in caves, too. The air inside the cave is warmer than the air outside, which helps to insulate animals from the cold.

The Virginia big-eared bat, an endangered species, hibernates in caverns in West Virginia.

Some scientists think that the deep sleep bears enter in winter is a type of hibernation.

(t) AFP/Getty Images/Newscom, (b) Juniors Bildarchiv/Alamy

If the glowworm detects a noise, it can turn off its light so that it can't be seen.

Farther into the cave is the cool, damp twilight zone. There is minimal light this deep in the cave, so green plants can't grow. Many of the creatures that reside here are troglophiles, or cave lovers. They may spend their whole lives in caves, but they can also survive in the outside world. Certain types of spiders, earthworms, beetles, frogs, and crickets are troglophiles.

Food in the twilight zone is not plentiful, and very little light is available. The animals living here can't rely solely on their sight to survive. They make use of other senses, such as hearing or touch, to help them locate the food they need and to find their way around. Their adaptations help them to cope with these specific conditions.

Another type of troglophile is the glowworm, which is the larva of an insect called a fungus gnat. One of its adaptations is the ability to illuminate its abdomen to attract prey. First the glowworm spins a web out of sticky droplets, then it switches on its light. The glowworm caches its tiny insect victims in the web until it needs a meal.

blickwinkel/Alamy

The New Zealand cave weta, a kind of cricket, lives in colonies on the undersides of cave roofs. It has particularly long **antennae**, which are up to seven times longer than its body. These antennae enable it to navigate and to feel around for food. Because of its tiny body and long, strong legs, this agile insect can leap more than 6 feet!

The New Zealand cave weta uses its extra-long legs to quickly leap out of harm's way.

ADAPTING TO SILENCE

In a place where food is scarce, it's useful to keep quiet! Instead of chirping, the African cave cricket can communicate in secret. It uses its wings to send out tiny, doughnut-shaped puffs of air, known as vortices. Although other cave crickets can feel these vortices, predators can't.

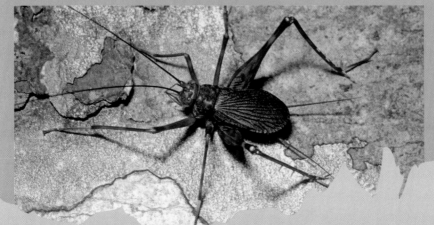

(t) Natural Visions/Alamy, (b) Premaphotos/Alamy

In a cave, how do animals get the **nutrients** they need? Plants can't grow in the dark, but plant-based nutrients are brought into caves in a variety of different ways. Rain and underground streams wash in twigs, leaves, seeds, and insects. The droppings of animals such as bats and cave crickets include recycled plant material. These are valuable sources of food for permanent cave dwellers.

Molds, **fungi**, and **bacteria** break down all this organic material and make it suitable for microscopic animals to eat. Although they are tiny, these microscopic animals are numerous. Larger cave dwellers eat them, and the larger animals are then eaten by other cave predators.

CAVE LIONS

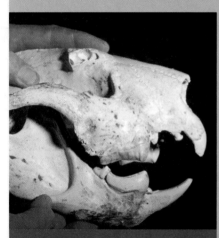

Scientists have been able to learn about these big cats from their very old bones.

Based on the ages of bones they have found, scientists believe that the European cave lion lived between 12,000 and 40,000 years ago. It was approximately 25 percent larger than today's lions. Although scientists think that it probably didn't live in caves and stayed above ground most of the time, it is called the cave lion because the bones of 14 of these animals were found in four caves in France.

Underground conditions often remain stable, and the skeletons of animals that die in caves can be preserved for a long time.

CLAY BRYCE/AFP/Newscom

CAVE FOOD WEB

The nutrients in guano, or bat droppings, and other materials are broken down and recycled as food by some cave creatures and microscopic organisms. These creatures are then consumed by larger predators.

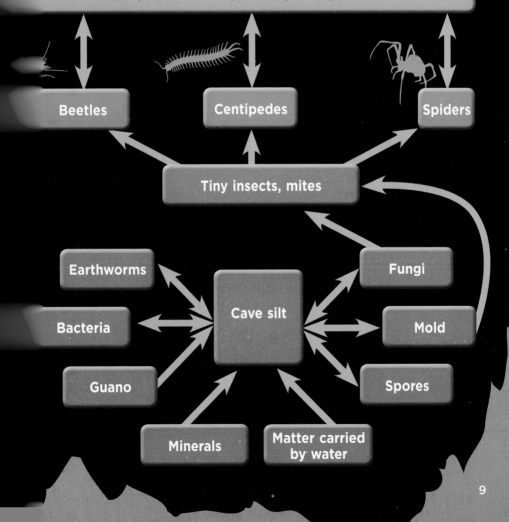

Bats

Frogs

Small insects, such as mosquitoes, gnats, glowworms, crickets

Beetles

Centipedes

Spiders

Tiny insects, mites

Earthworms

Fungi

Bacteria

Cave silt

Mold

Guano

Spores

Minerals

Matter carried by water

CHAPTER TWO

DARK AND SURPRISING PLACES

Imagine if you were transported deep underground into the heart of a cave—the area known as the dark zone. Here, far from the cave entrance, there is no light and no wind. No plants are growing. It is completely dark and silent, and the air is totally still. What would it take to survive in this environment?

Life in the Dark Zone

Animals that live permanently in this dark zone are called troglobites, or cave dwellers. They have all kinds of adaptations, such as small bodies, long limbs, and long antennae. Other adaptations are not so obvious, such as their ability to detect small vibrations or smells. Their adaptations help these creatures to move about safely and to forage and feed efficiently in a pitch-black environment where food is always scarce.

This insect, called a dipluran, has neither eyes nor wings, but it has long antennae and two tails.

Dante Fenolio/Photo Researchers/Getty Images

10

This pseudoscorpion has very long pincers but no need for eyes.

Many troglobites do not have the kinds of adaptations that animals above ground rely on for survival. For example, if you live your whole life in the dark, then eyes are not especially useful. Animals living in the dark zone typically have tiny eyes or no eyes at all.

In the world outside caves, most animals have coloring in their skin called pigment. Pigment is an adaptation that protects animals from the sun's rays or provides them with camouflage. However, pigment has no value in the dark zone of a cave. As a result, some troglobites have skin that is nearly see-through. Animals with adaptations that make them well suited to deep-cave life would probably not survive for long in the environment outside.

(t) Tom Hartman/Oxford Scientific/Getty Images, (b) Dante Fenolio/Photo Researchers, Inc.

This cave harvestman, or daddy longlegs, has long, thin legs and a tiny body. It is also blind.

THE ZONES OF A CAVE

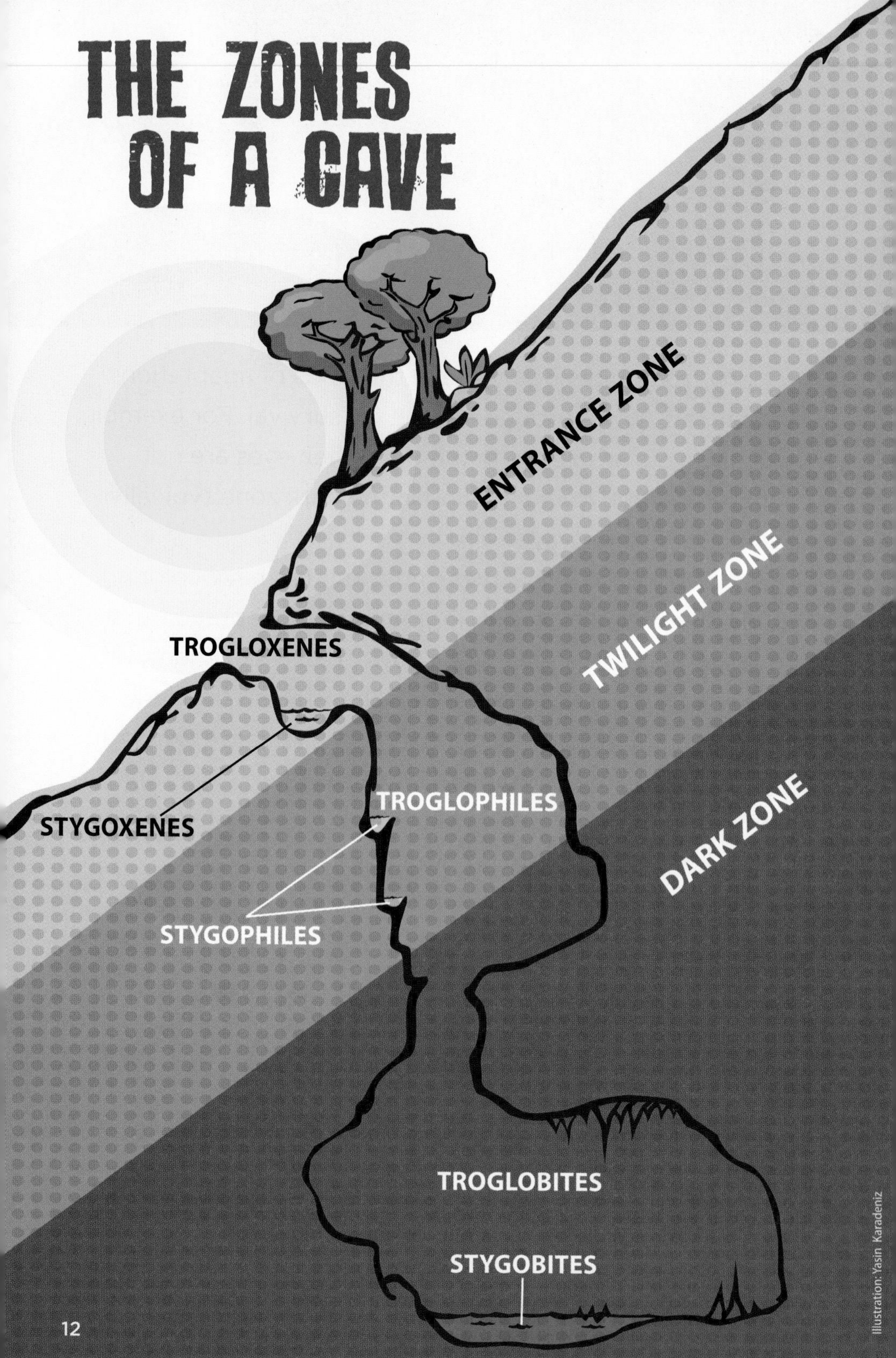

ENTRANCE ZONE

TWILIGHT ZONE

DARK ZONE

TROGLOXENES

STYGOXENES

TROGLOPHILES

STYGOPHILES

TROGLOBITES

STYGOBITES

Illustration: Yasin Karadeniz

Although it has no eyes, the Texas blind salamander can hunt by sensing its prey's movements in the water.

This cave crayfish has no pigment.

Aquatic Cave Dwellers

Creatures that live on land aren't the only cave dwellers. Many caves contain intricate networks of underground streams and ponds, some of which have specially adapted **aquatic** animals living in and around them.

Aquatic cave dwellers that can't survive outside the cave environment are called stygobites. Varieties of stygobite include blind, pale fish, salamanders without eyes, **translucent** crayfish, and other **crustaceans** that have no pigment.

The water that flows through underground caves usually enters from outside the cave and then flows out again. As it does so, it transports aquatic creatures into and out of the cave. Stygoxenes are aquatic visitors from above ground (perhaps carried there by accident). Stygophiles are cave-water lovers that may spend time outside the cave environment as well.

Sometimes water surges through cave systems, flooding passages, and dragging boulders. This can cause permanent changes to the underground environment, affecting the creatures that live there.

Extreme Cave Dwellers

Cave creatures have been unearthed in some unexpected places. In 2001, minuscule stygobites that resembled shrimps were discovered in limestone caves under the Western Australian desert. Because the caves are difficult to access, scientists stay above ground. They use fishing rods and nets to scoop up the tiny animals. A person fishing in the Australian desert would usually appear a little out of place. Now if you see someone doing that, you'll know why!

Some caves provide even more hostile conditions than a desert. These caves are too cold, too hot, or too toxic for most cave creatures to live in. Despite this, scientists have found specially adapted microscopic forms of life living in these places. Animals that are adapted to live in such extreme conditions are called extremophiles.

This scientist is fishing down a borehole for subterranean aquatic animals in the Western Australian arid zone.

Greenland's frozen ice caves are home to extremophiles.

Most animals could not possibly survive the frigid conditions in Greenland's ice caves. However, scientists have discovered microscopic creatures living there as well. These creatures have adapted to withstand the caves' sub-zero temperatures.

Mexico's Cueva de Villa Luz is another extreme cave environment. The cave emits fumes of hydrogen sulfide, a toxic gas that smells like rotten eggs. Scientists have given the microbes that live on this poisonous gas names such as snottites, blue goo, and slime balls! The scientists working in these caves need to carry gas meters so that they can monitor the level of gas and stay safe.

The extremophiles living in Mexico's Cueva de Villa Luz thrive on a gas that's poisonous to many other animals.

(t) moodboard/Alamy, (b) Stephen Alvarez/National Geographic/Getty Images

CONCLUSION

Cave creatures spend part or all of their lives in dark underground worlds that are vastly different from the bright surface world in which we live. Just as we couldn't survive for long in these harsh underground environments, many cave creatures couldn't survive in ours. The adaptations that equip them to live beneath the ground would make it dangerous for them to live above it.

How do we know which of the cave creatures' features are adaptations that have developed specially for cave conditions? And how do we learn how each animal's adaptations enable it to survive? We rely on scientists for answers to these questions. These scientists might be biologists, archaeologists, **paleontologists**, or geologists. Their research involves climbing, diving, rappelling, or squeezing into cold and dark caves. They observe and photograph cave animals to learn more about them.

Like all people exploring caves, scientists must take care not to disturb the fragile environment. They risk changing the conditions to which the cave creatures are adapted.

Mark Moffett /Minden Pictures/Getty Images

Because the animals living in the deepest parts of caves can't easily travel to another cave, scientists have discovered some unique and rare species. Sometimes scientists also bring organisms out from deep inside caves to the surface. The scientists mimic the conditions of the cave in their laboratories and examine the microscopic organisms in detail.

Scientists have found an incredible range of creatures in caves all around the world. There is still a great deal that we don't understand about these animals and their lifestyles. For anyone interested in exploring the underground world, there are still many things left to discover and many mysteries left to solve.

Robbie Shone/Aurora/Getty images

Respond to Reading

Summarize

Use the most important details from *Cave Creatures* to summarize the selection. Your graphic organizer may help you.

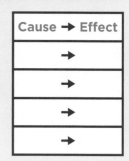

Cause → Effect	
	→
	→
	→
	→

Text Evidence

1. What text features help you identify *Cave Creatures* as an expository text? **GENRE**

2. Why do some cave dwellers have tiny eyes, no pigment, or extra-long legs or antennae? Look for causes and effects to find details that support your answer. **CAUSE AND EFFECT**

3. What does the word *hostile* mean on page 14? How do context clues in the paragraph help you figure it out? **PARAGRAPH CLUES**

4. Write about five different cave creatures and the kinds of adaptations they have for living in the underground environment. Describe each adaptation and how it helps the creature live in the cave. Use details from the text in your writing. **WRITE ABOUT READING**

Compare Texts

Read a folktale that explains why bats only fly at night.

Why Bat Flies AT NIGHT

One night Rat invited his old friend, Bat, over for dinner. "Oh, no!" thought Bat with a feeling of horror. "I'm going to be eating Rat's boring, flavorless stew for the seven-hundred-millionth time!" Even though Bat had given Rat a new cookbook for his last birthday, Rat still made the same old stew from his aunt's recipe. Bat had been served that stew for dinner time after time after time.

In those days, Bat walked everywhere. He walked very slowly from place to place. On the way to Rat's house, he came up with a cunning plan to get a little bit of flavor into his dinner.

"Rat!" exclaimed Bat when he arrived at last. "There's a competition for the best-flavored stew in the land. The winner gets a whole field of wheat."

"Fantastic!" said Rat. "I'll enter my stew."

"I know you don't like cooking with herbs, so here's another idea," Bat continued. "Your fur has such a lovely musky aroma—it's true essence of rodent. If you hop into the stew for a minute or two, it will become really tasty. You won't even need to change your aunt's recipe."

But the two friends hadn't thought very carefully about Bat's idea. They were so excited about improving the dish that they both forgot how hot the stew would be. Rat leaped into the simmering stew pot without delay. He leaped out again at once with an enormous scream.

Bat was very frightened. He ran for the door and tore home without sticking around to taste the stew!

Illustration: Barry Gott

The next day, Rat's aunt was very angry about what had happened. She took Rat to the king's court to complain. She thought that Bat had purposely played a mean trick on Rat. The king offered to give Rat some cooking lessons. Then the king ordered his soldiers to find Bat and bring him back to the castle to explain himself.

But the soldiers couldn't find Bat, who was hiding in a dark cave. Even when they came to search the cave, they couldn't see him—Bat was high above, hanging upside down from the cave roof.

From that day forward, Bat ventured out only when darkness fell. He swooped through the night, feasting on the freshest, juiciest insects. Bat was perfectly happy because the insects were so much tastier than Rat's stew!

Make Connections

Why do you think people made up a story to explain an adaptation of bats? ESSENTIAL QUESTION

From what you've learned in *Cave Creatures*, how close is *Why Bat Flies at Night* to the truth?
TEXT TO TEXT

Illustration: Barry Gott

Glossary

antennae *(an-TE-nee)* thin, sensitive feelers on an insect's head *(page 7)*

aquatic *(uh-KWAH-tik)* living in water *(page 13)*

bacteria *(bak-TEER-ee-uh)* very simple, single-celled organisms *(page 8)*

colonies *(KAH-luh-neez)* animals of the same type living closely together *(page 4)*

crustaceans *(kruh-STAY-shuhnz)* animals, such as crabs, that have hard shells instead of backbones *(page 13)*

fungi *(FUHN-gahy)* living things, such as mushrooms, that do not make their own food but absorb food from decaying matter *(page 8)*

haven *(HAY-vuhn)* a safe place *(page 2)*

labyrinth *(LA-buh-rinth)* a place containing lots of passageways and blind alleys *(page 3)*

nocturnal *(nahk-TUHR-nuhl)* active at night and not during the day *(page 4)*

nutrients *(NOO-tree-uhnts)* food that contains all that an animal or plant needs to live and grow *(page 8)*

organisms *(OHR-guh-ni-zuhmz)* living things *(page 2)*

paleontologists *(pay-lee-ahn-TAH-luh-jists)* people who study fossils *(page 16)*

translucent *(trans-LOO-suhnt)* see-through *(page 13)*

Index

Focus on Science

Purpose To explore the adaptations an animal would need to live in a cave

---

Procedure

 Step 1 Make a list of adaptations that enable cave-dwelling creatures to live underground. Use the text, as well as research from the Internet, to help you make your list. For which zone of the cave is each adaptation important? How does each adaptation help cave dwellers survive?

Step 2 Choose three zones found in a cave. Make a chart that has three columns. Label the columns with each of your chosen zones. In each column, list the kinds of adaptations an animal would need in order to live in that zone, such as changes to senses or skin pigment.

Step 3 Choose one of your adapted animals to illustrate. Label the adaptations and include a caption that describes the cave zone in which your animal would live.

Step 4 Present your adapted animal to your group.

Conclusion Compare the adaptations of your adapted animal with those of another creature that lives in the same zone of the cave. What is the same? What is different? Do you think animals really could adapt to living in your chosen zone? Why or why not?